OTHER BOOKS BY NORMAN FINKELSTEIN

POETRY

The Objects in Your Life

Restless Messengers

Track (Volume 1)

Columns: Track, Volume 2

Powers: Track, Volume 3

Passing Over

Scribe

Inside the Ghost Factory

Track (Complete)

The Ratio of Reason to Magic: New & Selected Poems

From the Files of the Immanent Foundation

CRITICISM

The Utopian Moment in Contemporary American Poetry

The Ritual of New Creation: Jewish Tradition and Contemporary Literature

Not One of Them in Place: Modern Poetry and Jewish American Identity

Lyrical Interference: Essays on Poetics

On Mount Vision: Forms of the Sacred in Contemporary American Poetry

Like a Dark Rabbi: Modern Poetry and the Jewish Literary Imagination

AS EDITOR

Harvey Shapiro, *A Momentary Glory: Last Poems*

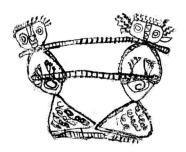

IN A BROKEN STAR

For David –

" And the letters rise up
and become a page "

Yours,

~~NORMAN~~
~~FINKELSTEIN~~

Norman Finkelstein

DOS MADRES

2021

DOS MADRES PRESS INC.
P.O. Box 294, Loveland, Ohio 45140
www.dosmadres.com   editor@dosmadres.com

Dos Madres is dedicated to the belief that the small press is essential to the vitality of contemporary literature as a carrier of the new voice, as well as the older, sometimes forgotten voices of the past. And in an ever more virtual world, to the creation of fine books pleasing to the eye and hand.

Dos Madres is named in honor of Vera Murphy and Libbie Hughes, the "Dos Madres" whose contributions have made this press possible.

Dos Madres Press, Inc. is an Ohio Not For Profit Corporation and a 501 (c) (3) qualified public charity. Contributions are tax deductible.

Executive Editor: Robert J. Murphy

Illustration & Book Design: Elizabeth H. Murphy
www.illusionstudios.net

Typeset in Adobe Garamond Pro & Beowulf 1
ISBN 978-1-953252-07-4
Library of Congress Control Number: 2020949776

First Edition

ACKNOWLEDGEMENTS

The author wishes to acknowledge the editors of the following journals, where sections of this book first appeared:

Marsh Hawk Review: "Memorial," "Escape Clause."

X-Peri: *The Adventures of Pascal Wanderlust* Book 1.

Aurochs: *The Adventures of Pascal Wanderlust* Book 2.

B O D Y: *The Adventures of Pascal Wanderlust* Book 3.

Dispatches from the Poetry Wars: *The Adventures of Pascal Wanderlust* Book 4.

IMAGES: The images in this book are details from Aramaic incantation bowls. These bowls, also known as demon bowls or devil trap bowls, were a form of ancient Jewish protective magic. They were usually inscribed in a spiral, starting from the rim and going to the center, with most of the inscriptions in Aramaic. A kind of amulet comprised of incantations written on earthenware, they were used by various Aramaic speaking communities during the Sasanian Mesopotamia period, approx. 224-651 CE. Often the incantations in the bowls were accompanied by graphic images which commonly depicted bound demons, as well as a variety of animals and abstract magical symbols or characters. The bowls were placed facing downward with the intention of capturing the demons, and were usually placed in the corner of the home of a recently deceased person, in courtyards, or in graveyards.

TABLE of CONTENTS

I

IN A BROKEN STAR

II

RETRIEVED DOCUMENTS

III

ThE ADVENTURES OF PASCAL WANDERLUST

... 21 ...

IV

ThE SONGS OF PASCAL WANDERLUST

I

IN A BROKEN STAR

In a broken star…

In a broken star
the words fall into the words

But the machine says
blow across my screen

And the letters rise up
and become a page

A page upon a page
crossing the centuries

The machine says look
and you will understand

Berlin

A tiny book…

A tiny book
in a space cut into

*A Foreigner Carrying
in the Crook of His Arm
a Tiny Book*

A miniature scroll
in a space cut into

*On Longing: Narratives
of the Miniature, the Gigantic,
the Souvenir, the Collection*

And on the gigantic canvas
dolls' dresses, girls' dresses

Or a figure impaled
by shards of glass
its head a tree of emanations

Berlin

A single girder…

A single girder
in the worn brick wall

Beneath the exposed
rusted column

The Eternal Lamp
found beneath the concrete

Marble fragments
faded golden stars

Berlin

house of names…

House of names
house of the dead

We walked out
into the sunshine

Walked into
the cemetery's shade

Whimsy and horror
photos and souvenirs

Prague

This is the truth…

This is the truth
the whole truth
holy and whole

Written in clay
that comes to life
comes into life

Fallen clay
fallen figure
comes and goes

From life into life

Prague

On Dohány Street…

On Dohány Street
a silver willow
in the fenced courtyard
past the graves

The guides in the sanctuary
speaking French
speaking Hebrew
regale the tourists

The puppet master
on all the billboards
tells us nothing
has really changed

Budapest

And vistas!...

And vistas!
eternal vistas
internal vistas
on which to brood

The sunlight on the rivers
bridges and palaces
cathedrals
on which to brood

Crowds on the banks
blood on the banks
eternal vistas
internal vistas

On which to brood

Budapest

Sometimes the poem...

Sometimes the poem
is a kiss upon the cheek
sometimes a blow
to the back of the skull

But the music there
is always perfect
in the ancient basement
or gilded hall

The cimbalom
and violin
in the ruin bars
and elegant restaurants

So that the poem wanders off
dazed by love
wounded by hatred
while the music plays on

Budapest

Ships and sultans…

Ships and sultans
triumphal cars
stags, satyrs
and goddesses enthroned

The musicians
and the cogwheels
behind the musicians

All come to life
with a golden key

The door opens

The peasant drops his pants
farts melodiously

While the arrows fly
the cannons fire
the centaurs charge

This purse is filled
with coins, with gems
—here comes the Devil!
better run away!

Vienna

We are all sepia…

We are all sepia
photos on a napkin ring

We are all on the stairwell
caught by the maid-servant

There are so many of us
here in the apartment

So many of us
in the crimson waiting room

"I was glued to the steps
and unable to budge from the spot."

Vienna

II

RETRIEVED DOCUMENTS

Memorial

The voices of the dead? That would be
one way of putting it. The records are unclear
on this point, and many are illegible, or have
yet to be deciphered. The illustrations indicate
that these machines—or organisms—were
intended to perform certain repetitive tasks,
and operated in the most hostile environments.
Even now, their sentience level shifts in response
to certain chronomorphic manifestations
which our instruments can hardly register.

An agent in the front of the apparatus
receives the stimuli but retains no trace of them,
while behind it there is a second agent
which transforms the momentary excitations
of the first agent into permanent traces.
If we replace these agents with systems,
then we must locate the primary system
at the motor end of the apparatus,
thus preserving the integrity of the structure
and the totalizing force of its design.

This is an atonement structure. One would
imagine them to be ubiquitous, but that
is by no means the case. In fact, insofar as
they are regarded as a supreme achievement
of self-building, they are relatively rare.
Safely contained, the violence of desire
is mourned, but never truly wanes.
Here it abides, becoming, if not its
contrary, then a useful, if not altogether
trustworthy, guardian. You have heard its song.

This structure appears unfinished, or it may
be a ruin. We are, after all, on a battlefield
of an ancient war—notched swords, dented
armor, feathers fallen from broken wings.
Memory, like a searchlight, momentarily
illuminates certain figures, certain events.
It is difficult to imagine the power released
by these engines, to say nothing of those removed
by the groundskeepers. Memory, like a black light,
momentarily causes certain objects to glow.

That is how they are captured.

Escape Clause

From the deep wells of solipsism to the Avenue
of the Bureaucrats, this is the neo-surgence
of the erotic hyper-real, erupting in the psyche,
erupting in the streets, explaining itself and freeing
itself of all explanation. The containment units
were never designed to work at such intensities.

The material is always beside itself, always
supplemental. You may say it should remain
hidden, buried, encrypted. You may say this force,
this expedition, goes nowhere or recedes into
a hazy distance, past tense, past tremulous, to a place
that is here and then gone. What did you expect?

Sea bird, white giant, five-sided entities from
beyond the stars. When the glaciers collapse
and fall into the polar sea, when you peer ahead
into the mists, when with a deafening roar, when
with absolute silence, you close the book and
put on a sweater—the old stories autocorrect

to the New Urbanism, the New Verbalism,
a failure of the dreamwork too vast to comprehend.
If you are unable or unwilling to accept this fate,
please join the line forming to the left. This escape
clause, this independent clause, this being below
the rank of the sentence, will avert the severe decree.

After the Briefing

More vocalization. More localization. But when
released into the water, it continues to grow.
Its influence spreads, and in the contest
of hither and yon, the advantage shifts to
the far side. Wishful thinking? Precisely.

These are only pen-and-ink drawings. The colorist
will complete the project at a later date. Very few
word balloons are necessary, for such is not
the way of this narrative, which depends upon
the structure of the frame, perspective, and scale.

The worshipful figures rise up from unknown depths,
assuming strange postures. But this communication,
sent from this particular communicant, refers to gifts
of another sort. And the degree of gratification
for all involved remains open to question.

I have been thinking lately of how, in the course
of things, the unaccountable disappearances
accumulate, take up more "space" in my memory,
so that my own "voice" becomes increasingly necessary
for articulating what is really a cosmic condition.

Imagine, then, how love is found, and lost, and found
again. Imagine, then, the rules, the procedures,
the organizations, all of which constitute an enormous
fantasy which pushes continuously against boundaries
erroneously thought to be real. Consider it giving way.

Strange Platforms

With this one he accesses the Talmud,
and with this one the entire run of The X-Files.
From a wardrobe of avatars, he selects
the ones least like himself—old beggarman,
blue limbed god, warrior princess—
but soon to be abandoned. Back again
to the mage, not the least, but not
the greatest of his order. When she comes
to him in a dream, he speaks so eloquently,
and with such obvious regret. They are under
the portico that was torn down in the renovation.
He speaks of his good fortune, of his family
and friends. He speaks of his fears as she
draws closer. He does not speak of his losses,
and at this point the sky above them
is replaced by a NASA photograph
of a black hole consuming a star.
Incalculable exchanges of energies,
incalculable loss of biomass. He dislikes
the one that is all mute images, though he
understands that they are not really mute.
The audio files of birdsongs, the archive
of flute players ancient and modern—he scrolls
past them. There is an instrument that measures
the percentage of quaintness, of kitsch, of cliché.
He no longer finds it particularly useful.

The Guide

Each little figure in its glass globe, hovering
near the ground or wildly swerving at a fantastic
speed, was a deadly threat. How they had managed
to avoid a direct encounter was nothing short
of miraculous. I am the guide. I am here
for the orphans, the wounded, all the lost ones.
I may bring you to safety, but there is nothing safe
about me. I am a lantern that casts no light,
I am a book that cannot be read. I will find you
and if you follow me, I cannot say where I will
lead you. When I came for them, it was too late
for her. Body intact, mind keen as ever,
but the spark, ah, the spark was already
ascending. Nothing to be done. She whispered
in the small one's ear, nodded to me, and down
the path we fled. I had to open a door. The strain
was overwhelming. In the end, only the letters
protected us. Golden birds on silver branches.

Mercurial hermeneutics? Of course. But they
were not entirely reliable. The child, on the cusp
of adolescence, would not settle, would not
stabilize. Turbulence. Agitation. Sheltering in
the cave, intent upon the shadows, seemingly
calm, she (he?) would suddenly bolt toward
the entrance, and have to be restrained. At those
moments, we shared a certain clairvoyance.
From great heights, I saw wheels and spheres,
pyramids and temples. I sat quietly at a table
among bookcases and charmed automata.

Darkness and stars. Woodland paths. Memories
are portents, portents memories; we see beyond,
look behind, but only so far. Let it go.
There are flowers at your feet, and a canopy
of sky above you. A child in springtime—
hard to believe! I wanted to give you my blessing,
but when I turned to you, you were gone.

III

ThE ADVENTURES
OF PASCAL WANDERLUST

*All of humanity's problems stem from
man's inability to sit quietly in a room alone.*

BOOK 1

1.

Pascal Wanderlust, flowered Docs
and mist-grey cloak, follows the ley line
leading down the lane. The last patches
of snow are melting, and Pascal side-
steps puddles on the way to palaces
lately dreamed. Breezes promise music,
scented sensuous turnings of air
and vapor, rustling sounds. Pascal
pulls back a hood grown moist
in greening weather. That Shining Land
lying just ahead, mirage at mountainous
horizon: what does Pascal know of destinations?

2.

Pascal considers the wanderer's destiny:
the homeless, the uprooted, the exiled,
those forced out upon the roads, lost,
cursed, unrecoverable, an uncountable
company. What of the hidden sinner,
the hidden saint? Pascal recalls
a mythy moment in a mythy mind.
Recalls a fall, recalls taking on a wanderer's
garb, recalls regarding a wanderer's fate
as one that may as well be accepted. Recalls
the road and the blessing of the road, recalls
willing exile among all the broken and unwilling.

3.

Behind the North Star, Pascal sees great shapes
moving in the polar night. These are signs.
These are airy nothings. These are "clusters
of cubes and planes," "the unknown arcana
of upper air and cryptical sky." These quotations,
thinks Pascal, ought to be taken seriously.
Allusion and immediacy, forever in conflict,
cancel each other out. Only the tone remains,
only the vaporous cadence, perceptible
yet mysterious, leading to completion of
the task. Completion? Behind the North Star,
Pascal stares into the void and does not blink.

4.

Wanderlust thinks of Eros, "conspicuous
and noisy enough," of their long friendship
on separate paths. At the crossroads one must
worship the god. "Fell down on my knees,"
the singer sang. What singer? What god? Eros,
thinks Wanderlust, considers himself a god,
sidesteps his fate, never finds himself at any
crossroad. Wanderlust, led by wanderlust,
recalibrates constantly, knowing doubt to be
the one assurance. Plucky Pascal, restless,
rests assured. Remembers the quiet of that
room. Remembers an inevitable departure.

5.

Pascal meditates upon ruins, visits battleground
memorials, heroes' graves. Pascal is unimpressed.
Verdigrised plaques mark historical events.
Pascal prefers the unrecognized, the clandestine,
the encrypted. The barrier thins out; the liminal
space expands. A free agent, Wanderlust moves in
and out, before and after. Puts on a suit, puts
on a dress, changes hairstyle in accordance
with the times. This happened, and then this.
Don't you believe it, thinks Pascal. Such skepticism
is foundational. I used to work there; then
I was laid off. Don't you believe that either.

6.

Pascal looks on as they emerge from the sea.
Perhaps on assignment, perhaps on vacation:
notes what is certainly a return of the repressed.
Wanderlust on the case! The uncle shot himself
and the grandmother leapt from the pier to be
welcomed far below. Webbing between stubby
digits, wreathed with seaweed red and brown.
Shameless Pascal at the keyhole, snaps shots
of college boys with voluptuous fishwives.
Someone at Miskatonic will pay handsomely for these.
Monstrosity. Hybridity. Alchemy. Figures lurk
in the shadows. Pascal catches a bus out of town.

7.

The man behind the desk regards Pascal
as a "person of interest." Pascal has no
regard for him at all. Longstanding foes,
they try to conceive of a world where one
or the other has disappeared. Should one
or the other disappear, what would
the remaining one do? Rainbow hued
Pascal, rendered in black and white, knows
he's watching. Knows of photos in a file.
As for the man behind the desk, this...person,
this Wanderlust, these suspicious blossomings
like roadside flowers—need to be contained.

8.

Pascal puts down the graphic novel and sighs.
Sexy and sincere, the author's on to some-
thing, but doesn't seem to have it quite right.
Behind the shades are eyes, not mouths and teeth.
The darkness and the fear of darkness dwells
in dream and comes forth to consume us.
No other power empowers us, much as we'd
like to believe. Or thwarts us. The man behind
the desk knows it. Wanderlust knows it too.
It's not the sort of knowledge one will find
in any book—or so it is written. Still, the man
behind the desk rarely removes his shades.

9.

Pascal in the Palace of Mirrors, flowered Docs
receding into bad infinity. Pascal in a morass,
spring blooms besmirched. Companions likewise,
lashing out in narcissistic rage. Pascal dodges,
returns the blow, sees blood and shards of glass.
Wounded self, wounded other. The man behind
the desk, voracious, watches on the screen,
feeding on enmity and strife. Let the mockers
mock. Let the idly curious mill about and gawk.
Whatever may be learned here is a mere reflection
of perennial doubt at a millennial pitch. Not for
the man behind the desk. He knows everything already.

10.

"If I am not for myself," reads Pascal—but can't
go on. Something is alive in the room, something
is there that should not be there. Studying *Avot*
at midnight may not have been a good idea. A sip
of wine—steady now! Pascal has heard of these
old ghosts, these antic moralists in grey and white.
"You are here alone? What are you?" Poor Pascal
has never had an answer. Unworthy Wanderlust,
unworthy of the name, unable to remain alone,
unable to be a self, unable to go forth and be
for others. Haunted Pascal at midnight, waiting,
watching for the dawn: "And if not now, when?"

11.

"Pascal Wanderlust to the Dark Tower came"—
and never mind the details of the quest. "Here it is,"
thinks Pascal. A great black bird sails overhead.
Neither knight nor childe, but a child of night,
Pascal, in the midst of dust and thorns, remembers
the fragrance of magnolia at warm spring sunsets.
A sheet of flame surrounds the Tower; faces peer
and bodies writhe. But Pascal has no peer. No one
does. Each one of us wanders toward a Tower;
each Tower has a door that may (or may not) open;
each member of the Band learns this, and hence
becomes a member of the Band. Wanderlust turns

12.

toward home. Wanderlust in a room alone,
writing parables. Wanderlust a parable, writing
to the end. One wins or loses, writes Pascal,
and as if under a spell, understands the wager
need not be placed at all. The infinite spaces
do not frighten me. I want to show you a new
abyss. Put on your boots and descend with me
into a place that is neither dark nor light. Are you
at home in this echoing immensity? Are you
secure in what we call your soul? I call to you,
soul, or else I call to nothing at all. I am in
a room alone, and it is toward you that I wander.

BOOK 2

1.

Through darklight, through vaporous clouds,
to the aether, Pascal Wanderlust ascends.
Darklighter, self-appointed demiurge, Pascal
scatters seeds, microbial offshoots, organic
sparks. Soul-seeker, soul-maker, resoled
Wanderlust, tendrils of hair creeping from
beneath the damp hood. What was seen
in the depths, what was done there? Exploits,
exploited for myths, expropriated by myth-makers
of uncertain date. Dateless time, thrown hopelessly
against history, against that obdurate wall.
Heeded. Seeded. *Watch how this grows.*

2.

Pascal and the Other: anti-archetype, lost
and found companion, alter-ego altered
and brought up from the abyss. Orphic
lover, Orphic alternative, Orphic mystery
seemingly solved. This is the good mirror,
thinks Pascal, this is the mirrored meeting,
these are the two that are one, singing
of love. So it seems, comes the echo, so
it always seems. When you wandered up,
flowered boots among the flowers, were you
dreaming of happy endings, were you
dreaming of love at all? And are you now?

3.

There were puppets and puppet masters. There were
armies of trolls. There were clubs and foundations,
associations and parties, in living rooms and backyards.
There was history, and there were history's losses,
history's erasures, histories of inevitability stretching
backward and forward, eternity glowing or glowering
in streets and darkened hallways. There were borders.
And there was Pascal Wanderlust, writing in a room,
writing in the past, writing in the present. Here is
Pascal Wanderlust, in the present and of the present,
witness and actor, acting as witness, Pascal
the historian, Pascal the agent, claiming agency.

4.

All the elegant instruments are cast aside.
In the stadium the anthems ring out, and in
the dive bar the drunks are singing. Pascal's
Other, anti-Wanderer, seeker sent forth, attends.
To whom? Someone in the crowd, at the rally,
at the all you can eat buffet, hungry soul talking
to himself while shouting with the others, or in
the bathroom with a needle in her vein. Vain
anti-hero, to think a presence could make
a difference. "Come back," reads Pascal's text,
"come back and tell me what we need to know.
Come back and tell us about the pain."

5.

Wanderlust awakens; the Other sleeps on. At dawn,
the wise and ancient insects begin to creak and chitter,
singing tragic songs. Lost lovers, lost children, harsh
realities leaching into dreams. This must be what
they mean by oneiric infection, a condition I was
never taught to prevent. No hope of a cure, shamanic
or otherwise. I was never properly schooled, but it
didn't seem to matter up till now. Now and in the
"foreseeable future" (head shaking under the hood),
the nightmares of the waking world are more than any
sleeping soul can bear. Pascal's Other turns and makes
sweet moan. A gentle kiss, and quietly, Pascal slips out.

6.

Pascal wanders up the little street, finds the
house number, reads the sign in the window:
"Dr. Augustus Sprechenbaum, Psy.D. Member
in Good Standing, 3 𓂀. Long & Short Term
Treatments Available. Psychic Wisdom On a Need
to Know Basis." Draws a deep breath. Knocks.
A young woman, scarcely out of her teens.
A corridor leading to a stuffy waiting room.
Tweed suit. Short white beard. A Siamese cat
yawns, stretches, settles back on the couch.
"Master, I have come…" begins Pascal, but
the old man raises his hand, shakes his head.

7.

"From Alexandria I went to Giza. No one knew the School
was still in operation. I don't know why they let me stay.
Stargazing, mostly. Some ventriloquism. Eventually I was
named an Adept. From there I set up shop in Prague.
Florence had little to offer, but Paris, and Vienna of course
—and Zürich! You'd be surprised. But about your problem
—what can I tell you that you don't already know? You see
a man indignant, hostile, enraged, but I see an infant crying out
in need. He hurls his misery at you. Can you contain it?
You grow miserable yourself. There are potions, incantations,
songs of experience. You know all the tunes. My dear, look
at those boots. This newest avatar suits you. Now go home."

8.

Obsessive Pascal, alone or in company, writes letters
that remain unsent, speechifies to imaginary audiences.
Take the old man's advice—if it is advice. Pascal,
prone to panic, prone to pursuing phantoms, spooked
by phantasms floating in the dark, collects traumas
as if they were souvenirs. Memories flood the soul:
the smoldering ashes of the great estate, the sky above
full of bright wings falling. What do they screen?
Betrayals. Accusations. Desires summoning desires,
the endless deferral of gratification. Pascal calls out
to that questing Band, that ecstatic Company, hears
them call back the name that names the task: *Darklighter*.

9.

Pascal studies the harsh argot of crows,
the jabbering jargon of jays, the oral law
of owls. Fluent in the Esperanto of gulls,
raised hearing the mothering coo of doves,
Wanderlust wonders why the blackbird's
melodies, the lark's light airs, have yet
to find their way into the codex. Upper limit
music, lower limit speech: Wanderlust
wants none of it. No range or sliding scale,
an infinite interdimensionality constitutes
the nested totality. Out of the marsh of a
lonely mind, a red-winged blackbird sings.

10.

In a dream, Pascal searches down a maze
of corridors, through randomly opening doors.
A friend imprisoned, a favorite jacket missing,
spectral breath, slow-motion panic. Pascal
wakes: fallen world, mediated world, peopled
by hungry ghosts, populated by robot voices,
endless boasts, endless lamentation. Pascal
wakes: speaking Hypnos, speaking Oneiric,
casts spells in ancient tongues, plays the long
game because there is no choice. Ghostly
laughter: what are you doing, what are those
words you mumble? Time bombs, says Pascal.

11.

The occult explosion changes everything.
It releases fantasmic energy, and all that dwells
in overheated imaginations comes alive
in the material world. The magicians dabbling
in nuclear science, the physicists practicing
the necromantic arts, the poets and painters
providing templates and archetypes, updated
in an instant, caught in a temporal loop.
An alternate reality. Ever dissatisfied, Pascal
considers the well-appointed cell, looks out
the window to the street below. No monstrous
hybrids, no barricades. No wizards. No

12.

revolutionaries? There is a fire that burns
in everything: so teaches the hermit in
his cell, the wandering scholar beneath
the trees. Depart from yourself and you
will know it in every molecule of your
being. It is always the telling of the telling,
song sung in a hereafter that always lies ahead.
I don't believe it, says Pascal, at a desk
in the study or following the ley lines in
the meadow. Hears thunder on the ridge,
shots in the street. Tightens the laces of
flowered Docs, pulls the hood down low.

BOOK 3

1.

Symbols and tables, charts and graphs,
elements and molecules, the atom and
the Adam. Fire and flood, vandals and
acts of God, the library in ruin, the floor
of the laboratory littered with broken glass.
Spirit photos and dream-visions, drones
hovering outside of windows and portals
opening above pentagrams inscribed in
chalk. Lightning flashes, camera flashes,
sounds of a lute in earbuds, of a bar band
echoing in the heavens. Spells assembled
from random bits of data. Pascal logs on.

2.

Wanderlust among the automata: designs
by Pierre Jaquet-Droz, by Thomas Kuntz,
the cams controlling gestures forth and back
in space and time: The Writer, a cherubic boy,
eyes shifting as the hand indites; The Alchemyst
in his Clock Tower, reciting a spell as fires
spark and leap. Passions mechanized, reason
infused with wonder. Pascal in the machine:
the wandering witness, watcher reluctantly
thrust forward to act again and again. Re-
member when it was you writing on little
cards? When fire leapt at your command?

3.

Pascal drops a quarter in the slot,
and the Gypsy Queen shuffles the deck.
The turbaned head nods, and Pascal
recalls the old balladeer among the Buddhas
and statuettes of Bast. Fish cakes with romaine
leaves, vanilla ice cream from Schrafft's.
Soon a child would come, got as a meteor
flashed across the sky, bearing a charm.
The gears turn, the eyes open, the hand
proffers a card. A wind is blowing from
the bottom of the world, calling Pascal
to come away. What card is this? The Fool.

4.

The aero hovers briefly above the calving
glacier before shooting toward the interior.
Mountains upon mountains. "The wind is too
strong," shouts Peter to Wanderlust. Pascal
points out the spot. A Kugelmass Projector.
"Keep the book open *and don't turn the page.*"
"The stabilizers can't keep her steady for long."
Pascal nods. Boots on the ground. Cyclopean
architecture. Eldritch archetexture. Albino
penguins. "*Get out of there,* signals Pascal
"*—and close the book!*" Peter straps in his
dog. Full throttle. *Tekeli-li! Tekeli-li!*

5.

Wanderlust comes to. Blood-soaked hood,
torn cloak, bare feet. A stone slab in a dark,
closed space. The air warm, fetid. Far off,
a droning chant, punctuated by an almost
intelligible buzz. Hand gingerly touching
forehead. The slime has sealed the wound.
What next? Pincers, tentacles, brains in
jars. Interplanetary flights. It doesn't look
good for our hero, thinks Pascal. I've read
this book before. The nerdy boy in a corner
of the library, the goth girl in her bedroom,
painted black. Where are my boots? Aha.

6.

Consider the map, and note the pattern
of sightings. A former operative reports
that through a combination of chronopoesis
and narrakinetic techniques, a portal has
been opened into a previously inaccessible
textual continuum. Now consider how little
we know about the tellers of such tales,
to say nothing of the tales themselves.
When a hermeneut insinuates himself
in the discourse, sets up shop, as it were,
in some side street, it appears to stabilize
the meaning. It seems familiar. But no…

7.

Back at home, Pascal—
Back at headquarters, Wanderlust—
The tension is palpable. It's not easy,
being alone in two places at once. It's not
easy, being two at once alone. Such contradictions
invariably call for interpretation. Infection. Invasion.
Pascal Wanderlust at the Mountains of Madness finds
that the Other has been spirited away. Pascal Wanderlust
suspects that the Mountains of Madness are the home
and headquarters of the Other, whose spirit has fled
away. Pascal the alien, for whom nothing is alien,
finds the spirit headquartered at home.

8.

Lost Other, lost double, lost twin: Pascal
applies for aid at the Administration of Dreams.
"Can we help you?" In this sphere, if repetition is
the iron rule, then what help is there? "Oh, do not
despair! There are many ways to attend upon the world's
wound. We may not be the instrument of restoration,
but we can provide a guide to the perplexed.
In some instances, we suggest a partnership,
extend membership, offer employment.
The seeker may become the one he seeks. You
seem ideally suited. Your experience speaks for
itself. Besides, you have the look we want."

9.

The lesser moon rises above the silent barrens.
Pascal Wanderlust, reclusive recruit, wipes
chalky dust from flowered Docs, looks out
to the horizon, where crags like broken teeth
complete the view. This is the nadir of the soul's
journey, this is the outer rim where all your
wandering turns in upon itself and ends. Here
histrionics halt, hysteria softens into silence.
And yet you were sent here to monitor dreams!
Whose dreams? Your own? For surely you are
alone here, beneath the lesser moon. And when
the greater moon rises, shedding more light—

10.

what then? In the dream, Pascal is divided
once more, man and woman facing each other,
and a darklight void is opening between them,
there on that dusty plain. From the distant peaks
come winged monstrosities, circling, swooping
in the pestilential air. They hear a voice cry
*The dead are entitled to interpret the dream
however they wish!* The gulf is widening.
Above them the sky opens to reveal its internal
mechanism, its cogs and wheels, the plasma
of space, the tissue of dreams. Snowflakes fall
like stars, warm, comforting. Welcome home.

11.

"Dear Bruno: I—we—cannot thank you enough.
It was really touch and go there for a while.
I had forgotten that you had been appointed
Celestial Mechanic. I'm amazed that you've
managed to keep your post amidst all this turmoil.
The words are paths down which we wander
into a lost world. The words are a fantastic
vehicle, part carriage, part telescope, part
camera taking pictures of where we have been,
where we are going. You and all who work
in that department, governing orthodoxies,
heresies, you machinists of terrors and comforts—

12.

no, we cannot thank you enough." Pascal sighs
and puts down the pen. Those strange, fleeting
moments of renunciation and regret. They never
last long. And the imagined dangers, the rescues,
the lost companions, mentors, opponents human
or otherwise—this Wanderlust, wandering
perpetually to and with the Other—did you
volunteer for this service sometime long ago,
or did it come to you in the mail, like a pair
of boots you didn't recall ordering, but somehow
knew you were fated to wear? Perhaps it no longer
matters. Here is a stamp for your letter. A flower.

BOOK 4

1.

Like a pilgrim on the way to a secular shrine,
Pascal Wanderlust negotiates the contradictions.
This is the not-me: in its grey uncertainty,
the landscape observes itself among fog-wrapped
hills. Pascal hesitates: what else to describe?
This is the good-me: the sun shines down upon
the ley lines, and the mists evaporate as the path
is revealed. Secure Pascal, the system secured,
is happily received into the steady state. *Wake up,
Wanderlust!* These operations are never secure.
The steady state is an illusion—unbound energies
remain at play. Can you restore the balance?

2.

In a dream, Pascal hears the sound of a horn.
Azure, azure: the scales appear in the heavens.
Astraea astray, and Wanderlust in no condition
to find her. The psycho-political muse refuses
her attentions. Is the quest then stalled? In
a dream, Pascal again beholds "the starry
dynamo in the machinery of night." Thinks of
prophecy and its costs. Wandering heroes,
wandering seers, extravagant tales told out of
school. "Creeds and schools in abeyance"?
Better stay in that room while it's still available—
but look out the window at the darkening sky.

3.

Pascal entertains guests from afar. Aliens,
members of a different Order, they agree
to hold a grand Consultation. Pascal adjusts
the trodes on the Universal Translator, pours
another cup of tea. *Wanderlust Unlimited,
Consultants.* The staticky hum of laughter
from organs intended for entirely different
purposes. Partial materiality despite appearances
to the contrary. Pascal reflects, straightens up.
Viscous matter on the teacups. This partnership
might not be such a great idea. In any case,
the carpets and furniture will have to cleaned.

4.

Guest. Ghost. Host. Not all the visitors
materialized, nor spoke so as to need
translation. A shadow in the corner
of the room, in the corner of the eye.
An enigmatic, ectoplasmic smile:
"Pascal, it's not an accident that Din
and Hesed stand opposed and balanced
on the Tree. You know this. All the star-
born do. Yet who can bring them together
along the pathways of their power? Who
bears such adornment as may in Tiferet
dwell?" *Real old school,* thinks Pascal.

5.

Mentor or maggid, here or hereafter, she had taught
Pascal all that was necessary. Every triumph, every
disaster. Diplomacy and alchemy. Statecraft and
witchcraft. Clandestine meetings and sudden
apparitions, romantic songs and necromantic chants.
And after her return, when it all came down, when
the golemancy failed and the armies of homunculi
stormed the estate, the chain reaction obliterated
every unit, every outpost, and she and the soul
who would be reborn as Wanderlust fled on foot,
until she fell behind and refused to go further—
only then did Margaret tell Pascal her name.

6.

Pascal opens a portal—then closes it.
Pascal peers into a mirror—then looks
away. No Summerland for Wanderlust,
no sojourns in Faerie. Was it only yester-
day or the day before, or was it uncounted
moons ago, when Wanderlust, abandoned
on the outer rim, vowed never to go beyond
the limits of that double being, the psychic
range of that uncanny name? But who was it
who named you, Pascal Wanderlust? Was it
not she who first sent you forth? "There are
no limits," she whispers; "neither in your room

7.

nor on the starry path." So Wanderlust ascends—
"Past Midnight! Past the Morning Star!" Her Voice
rushes by in the wind. The *tzinorot* beckon.
Each Face gazes outward as Wanderlust approaches.
These are the boundaries of the infinite spaces,
the non-Euclidean forms, studied in Antarctica
and Provence. Elder Things hanging with Shimon
bar-Yochai among the hills of Galilee. *L'cha Dodi!*
The throbbing in Pascal's temples is more painful
now as the Book opens, floating in the silent void.
The Zohar, aka The Necronomicon. Sacred fantasy.
Drawings by Steve Ditko. Story by Stan Lee.

8.

Pascal on "the little pathway between speech
and silence," flowered Docs reflecting light
from distant stars. The delegation approaches.
Pascal would rather be at home, but business
is business—and look at the fire falling from
those wings! A memory descends, even as they
descended upon the cliffs of Schloss Duino,
lifetimes ago. With whom are we consulting?
Will wonders never cease? Wondering Wanderlust,
witness and messenger, suddenly sees the terms
of this election. Aliens and angels abounding!
Pascal listens, turns off the Translator. עִבְרִית

9.

Purified Pascal recalls the hand that held
the tongs, the tongs that held the coal, the coal
upon the lips. Prophetic Pascal called upon
to speak. Reluctant Wanderlust, accompanied
by a host of proclaimers, all sent forth upon
missions which they have been forbidden to
reveal. Recite as you have been instructed—
and who shall receive instruction in turn?
Those who yet may turn. Wanderlust among
those who would be masters of turning, but to
what end? Poised between justice and mercy,
unpurified Wanderlust breaks rank, departs.

10.

Not the first messenger betrayed by the message,
not the first witness traduced by the testimony.
Not the first anchorite, not the first knight errant,
not the first soul suffering and celebrating division.
Not the first renegade, not the first revolutionary
accused of fomenting counter-revolution. Not
the first fugitive fleeing the state, not the first
passenger in flight forever. Not the first to simply
dream of escape, and in escaping, discover
a destiny: messenger, witness, anchorite, knight
errant, revolutionary, fugitive, passenger—
and guide. This is the way, says Pascal. Onward.

11.

The Florentine's Angelic Rose is seen in the skies
over Providence. Nephilim and Blengigomeneans
heed the call to arms. The letters leap from the scrolls.
Nice, thinks Pascal, adjusting the lenses. Phantoms.
Phantasmagoria. Phanopœia. Consults grimoires
and epic poems, refines the optics further. Mixes
a soundtrack: horns echoing among the hills, radio
static resolving into spacey theremin oscillations,
purgatorial cries—all in a minor key. Unsanctioned
interplanetary prophecy. Time to upload these visions,
broadcast these seeds. Worth the risk, thinks Wanderlust.
Tinkers with the motherboard. Boards the mothership.

12.

Twenty thousand leagues or light-years:
the steampunk extravagance of the *Nautilus*,
the *Pequod*'s ivory savagery, the sleek bridge
of the *Enterprise* with all its blinking lights,
the *Aero Rondo* Pascal piloted in a different
life—even those flowered Docs that take you
where you want to go…Wanderlust looks down.
The road is paved with pages, screens line
the path. Beyond, space folds and unfolds in
endless patterns too complex to be graphed.
Pascal picks a card, plots a course. Wanderlust
looks up. Locks. Wheels. Stars. Flames.

BOOK 5

1.

Wanderlust steps through the pages of the messianic
comic book, and stands before the statue of Lincoln.
An enormous golem at rest after his labors. Hundreds
of morons taking selfies, while Pascal stands in the
corner and weeps. Reads the writing on the wall:
*insurgent agents were in the city seeking to destroy it
without war.* How we have fallen. Wanderlust descends.
Nineteen more golems stand in the mist, wrapped
in ponchos, haunted and determined. When will it end?
King looks out across the Tidal Basin, wrapped
in stone glory. Pascal steps through again, and bathes
in the light of the Throne of the Third Heaven. Glory.

2.

Waves of indifference wash over Wanderlust,
worse than any hatred or hostility. For every
work rescued, how many are lost? How many
times must the heart give out, must the dream
find form, only to evaporate? Hooded Pascal,
cloaked in mist, robed in ritual, mythopoeic
personage, palest persona: among monuments,
museums, archives, temples to memory, upon
what mission, Wanderlust, do you now set out?
What forgotten passage would you restore? From
the dark haunts of oblivion, waiting patiently,
what object longs to rest cherished in your hands?

3.

A scroll, a gem, a ceremonial dagger,
an intricate clockwork to tell the future
by way of the past—none of this proves
in any way adequate. And the Great Work,
the Alchemical Marriage, the Androgyne
in whom you place your faith—that too
proves unsustainable. Out of what
substance have you built yourself,
and out of what sights, exotic and
mundane, have you built this shifting
set? Cloud-capped towers from which
wizards and poets peer down? Look closer.

4.

Too much tourism in the supernal realms
leaves even the greatest adepts exhausted.
A ban on Astral Travel might be good
for the soul, thinks Pascal, might encourage
greater concern for all the little, neglected
details supposedly crying out for more
attention. Everyday magic. Every day,
magic goes unnoticed. Unnoticed, things
appear and disappear, willed or unwilled,
and in their yearning so to be, they reappear
—perhaps too late. We await the final word,
thinks Wanderlust. May it never come.

5.

But the objects cry out. They always have,
they always will, even when there is no one
left to hear them. A million species lost
to oblivion, while these dumb, beautiful
ministers testify to the stars. Pascal steps back
from the shew-stone. How many times will
the demands of your art, the power of your
agency, raise you up only to let you drop,
broken by that terrible knowledge? On the
sidewalk, folks staring at those boots and
cloak, Wanderlust recalls a message from
that cunning operative, hidden in plain sight:

6.

"Much Madness is divinest Sense - " And what
but that desire for *tikkun olam* leads us to such
madness? And what but that longing for divinest
sense leads us to compose these spells and
incantations? Break the line and syncopate
these monotonous chants! Do away with all
this magic and reinstate—what? *Beware,
Wanderlust!* You've been handled with a chain
before. Your double soul, the beloved Other,
this fantasy of enchantment, enchantment of
fantasy, structure of rime—the Order to which
you belong offers only so much protection.

7.

But it will have to do. Floods, fires, deserts
spreading, oceans rising: nothing abolishes
chance, nothing abolishes human stupidity.
So be it. Sages and mages confer. Pascal
holds forth upon the Four Principles, the Two
Antinomies: male and female, containment
and extravagance. Debates with Eros there-
upon. Measure the music of the spheres?
Good luck with that. Some mysteries must
remain mysteries. Impart your wisdom,
Eros, partial as it may be. There is always
a surplus, bound to take us beyond. Immeasurable.

8.

Immeasurable! The very word is like a bell,
or better yet, a door into yet another elemental
world. Pascal suffers from cosmogonic angst,
an occupational hazard, with symptoms first
observed by the most ancient members of
the guild. What to do? No more consultations
with Dr. Sprechenbaum. No more psychic
journeys, no more visits to the outer rim.
The house next door is haunted: there's a trap
door in the basement floor; the attic window
offers views of perilous seas. Music echoes
in the living room: flute, hurdy-gurdy, violin.

9.

And yet it's still the house next door: one only
has to climb the front porch steps and knock.
The friendly old couple and their grandchildren,
visiting for the summer: Genevieve (eleven),
Felix (going on nine). She admires your boots;
he longs for a hooded cloak, as the afternoon
sun gives way to evening chill. It's pleasant
to linger with them in the garden—so polite,
so delighted with your tales. Wanderlust,
you fool, have you forgotten the significance
of such a pair? Just what do they desire?
What do their childish charms disguise?

10.

Demonic, soul-eating kids from some cheesy
horror film? Really? Pascal recalls a visit
to the workshop, a look at the alembic where
it all began. A bit of this, a bit of that, says
Margaret, smiling. Her lips brush the child's
forehead as she adjusts the cloak. Another
memory. One day, Wanderlust tells them,
these may be yours. For now, keep practicing
your instruments, and don't stray too far
into the woods. Or do so, for it may be time.
Parent and child, sister and brother, lover to
lover goes. The alembic bubbles on the fire.

11.

Not the children then but the memories
that they conjure: there lies the danger!
How much of your origin can you bear
to learn? Young Pascal, young Wanderlust,
walk with Margaret in the woods of the estate.
How delightful is the breeze in the shade!
Outside the barrier, many agents have fallen.
Emma has been trapped in the Summerland,
and cannot return. The next day Margaret
will prepare the compound. And all of this,
thinks Wanderlust, watching Genevieve
read to Felix, is itself nothing but a screen.

12.

The stories we tell ourselves to keep going,
and the objects to which we cling, long after
they are gone. The days we lost in the forest,
lost in the forest of days. The fragmentary past,
the fragments from which we make the past.
The wisdom we fail to achieve, the wisdom
of failure. I was a child, thinks Pascal, we were
two children, thinks Wanderlust. In the story,
we were lost in the forest, in the fragments
of the past. They failed, and so they grew wise.
And what have I done with this wisdom, asks
Pascal Wanderlust. What can I ever do?

BOOK 6

1.

Pascal sits drinking in the Tavern of the Magi.
Cupbearers come and go. That could have been
me. Perhaps, in a former life, it was. There are
truths to be found at the bottom of the wine cup,
but these are not the ones I seek. Union with
the Beloved? No more! cries Wanderlust. None
of the other drinkers bats an eye. The musicians
play one last number. Closing time, says the Host.
Here? mumbles Pascal. Now? But this is the
center of— Not for you, friend, says the Host.
One for the road? asks Pascal, forlorn. I don't
think so, he replies. You're too far gone already.

2.

Cosmogony recapitulates genealogy. You're drunk,
"friend," thinks Pascal. But what if that were the case?
Divine twins, kingdoms ruled by incestuous brothers
and sisters, devouring parents, mythic arguments over
lines of descent. Planets are born, revolve, fall into
the sun and die. My errands have sent me through more
than enough black holes. I've met myself coming and
going, flowers on black fields or white. I've debated
the scribe who writes in black fire upon white, and I am
weary to death of all I have been called upon to imagine.
Each of my senses magically enhanced, each of my
thoughts theurgically projected. A myth. A cosmos.

3.

No! I am not Adam Kadmon, nor was meant to be:
so have I been told, repeatedly. All that training,
all these adventures: perpetual journeyman, perpetual
wanderlust consuming an otherwise stationary soul.
Enantiodromia! Between a storybook past and a
dystopian future, Pascal feels the psychic tremors,
shudders at the loss of control. Who brought the sun
and the moon together? Their light was captured
and passed through the alembic, charging the bodies
within. In Margaret's file, Pascal beholds Dee's
hieroglyphic monad: the sun, the moon, the planets.
All of the virtues. All of the powers. One vessel.

4.

From which the ghosts come to drink—a perpetual
return. Is that how it's organized? A perpetual
going forth—is that it? This agitation, this longing
for rest, but always this hunger, calling forth itself
and its opposite. You say it is because there are
two souls within you, you point to your unbelievable
origin, you claim to remember and then you don't.
You are a hero. You are a sacrifice. You step back,
only to find your story written in a book that has always
been there on the shelf. Was it in in the library? The
laboratory? The office? The chapel? Doesn't matter.
You broke in and stole it, as they knew you would.

5.

Because you have always known yourself to be
a thief. Mercurial, hermetic, the secretive, ever-
changing sign appears on the surface, hinting
at the depths. The message is encrypted, and you
challenge them to decode it, to break into the crypt.
What they find has been dead a long time—do they
know the spell to return it to life? Would you teach
them the words? It is the words themselves that
you have stolen. It is they who must return from
the dead. What is that flower drawn upon your boots?
The asphodel. You have wandered long in those
ghostly fields, feeling no pleasure or pain. Come back.

6.

Wanderlust takes the new express from Innisfree
to Innsmouth. Settles into the cushy seat. Please
enjoy our complimentary Wi-Fi. Old-fashioned
Pascal prefers telepathy, tunes in expecting messages
from the beyond. Comes up with nothing but static.
The maggidim have been strangely silent. They have
nothing to say in the face of self-doubt. Negative
capability? Magic, they insist, is an art of the will.
So what will you do now? Wanderlust walks along
the strand, looking out to Devil Reef. An old friend
swims in for a brief visit. Stares at Pascal coldly.
"Nice to breathe the air of upper earth now and then."

7.

"Pascal Wanderlust is nothing but trouble! Sorry,
but that's what great-great-grandmother said to me
before I left. *Tries to right the balance and upsets it
every time. I told them the design was flawed ten
thousand years ago, but why listen to us? We dwelt
in the Abyss before the Beginning. What do we know?*
And honestly, Pascal, all those Miskatonic researchers
following your last visit. Former Foundation agents,
every one. Take some advice from an old school chum.
You were a goth with eyeliner and your first pair of Docs.
I was a rich kid from Ohio obsessed with my ancestry.
I learned I could change—the hard way. You can too."

8.

All too true. Pascal orders a bowl of chowder
and a local brew, malty sweetness overlaid with
a hint of seaweed. The waitress smiles, recalling
that last visit. Pascal would just as soon forget.
How many clever antics look like blunders now?
A local troubadour tunes up, covers an old song,
messing with the words: *Oh Lord, trapped in
Innsmouth again!* No more old haunts, and enough
advice from well-intentioned friends. "If the young
man had believed in repetition, of what might he not
have been capable? What inwardness he might have
attained!" But Pascal Wanderlust is no young man.

9.

Inwardness and outwardness: Pascal's room and
Wanderlust's adventures. An external hard drive
holds all the files pertaining to the Oberon Project,
though much more has disappeared. Histories
and analyses cram the shelves. Pascal knows all
about it: required reading, courtesy of Margaret.
What Pascal never understood was why the work
became so urgent. "The lovers had to be rescued,
they kept passing through each other": that was
the story released to the press. It was far worse.
Simultaneity broke out uncontrollably; dream
leakage could not be contained. The inside

10.

threatened to consume the outside. The Directors,
in their pride, refused all offers of aid. From then on,
the Foundation lost its credibility—its *believability*.
No wonder, in the end, the defenses all collapsed.
And there was young P.W., as the gardener called
the apprentice. Yes, there was young P.W.—running
for life. And never stopped running, or so it appears.
Hiding yourself away among your books, sending
yourself forth on adventures, shod and cloaked in
old mythologies but still trying to make it new.
Outer *and* inner, tradition *and* novelty: such a
magick spell would take a Faerie King (or Queene).

11.

And why bother to seek for balance? What
constitutes restoration? Do we imagine
costumed heroes fighting for *tikkun*?
What, wonders Wanderlust, does it even
look like? Sefirot floating in the void? Too
many fantasies and New Age guidebooks,
and you find yourself writing your own.
Pascal opens the window, lets in some air.
Lets in—a raven? a dove? Each carries
a note in its beak. Drops it on the desk.
Departs. I'm not sure if I should read these.
I'm not sure if they're meant for me at all.

12.

Dear Recipient: the bearer of this letter is Pascal
Wanderlust, of whom you may have heard. There
may be two such bearers, there may be one, or there
may be none at all. This letter may be accompanied
by a second letter, or perhaps Pascal Wanderlust
appears before you without introduction. Regardless,
there is something you must know, something Pascal
Wanderlust must tell you. We ask your patience and
forbearance in this regard. This letter has come a long
way, and has been the subject of many outlandish
adventures, which Pascal Wanderlust may be disposed
to relate. If this proves true, we beg your attention.

IV

THE SONGS
OF PASCAL WANDERLUST

In the library of books
that have never been written
I discovered the story
of Pascal Wanderlust

I discovered that I
was the author of the book
that my name appeared
on the title page

It was then I took the name
Pascal Wanderlust
it was then that I became
the story of myself

The story went forth
and the story returned
there were sights to see
and people to meet

Until the tale ended
to be returned to its shelf
in the library of books
that have never been written

Ever and never my songs
Darklight on the sea
Portal in the sky
Wound in the side of the world

What I saw upon the hill
What I saw in the deeps of the wood
What I saw in the deeps of the sea
Never and ever my songs

At the turn of the year
At the turn of our fate
At the turn of our song
Turning forever

Turning into silence
Somewhere behind the stars
The figures turning
Falling upon the earth

Falling and falling
Forever received
Falling into song
Falling silent

You come to a place
that mirrors a place
echoes a place
mourns a place

You leave a place
leading to a place
calling to a place
that may be a place

Where is the place
where you may learn of a place
a lost place
no place?

When you arrive at the place
you will know the place
you will learn in that place
that you are the place

It cannot be uncanny
because there is no home
no one home
no home at all

Look through the window
who is there
sitting in that chair
no one at all

Stranger to myself
myself my twin
look through the window
no home at all

Sitting in the chair
in empty air
myself my twin
no one at all

A talisman
worn over the heart

A talisman
taken to heart

Take heart
for here is a talisman

Heart
take heart

Approach the Throne
upon your knees
light bulbs and tin foil
and angels' wings

There in the garage
the rent unpaid
the secret light
for all to see

FEAR NOT
for this is true
inscribed in a notebook
inscribed on the sky

FEAR NOT
but approach the Throne
among faceless angels
there in the garage

I weep for the beauty
weep for the futility
the loss of futurity
for which we are guilty

the ceaseless disparity
endless monotony
death of melody
shattered unity

The bed at dawn
and the sun through curtains
The wind through curtains
in the gathering dusk

A figure seen through a window
Is it you my love is it me?
Is it me my love is it you?
Tell me before it is gone

Tell me before I am gone
before I find I am elsewhere
before I find I am other
than who I think I may be

Tell me before we must flee
Is it me my love is it you?
And we go where we must go
Do what we must do

Like phantoms caught
in a phantasmagoria

Like grim figures
inscribed in a grimoire

Like planets assigned
to a single symbol

Earthly hopes
cast out among the stars

I wander about
among the nurseries of stars

I wander the fields
where the planets are born

Earth is a cinder
a speck of ash

The souls extinguished
the firmament gone

I and my Other
can no longer dream

We were bound to this world
but are now released

I and my Other
a dream of fire

The Last Dream of Fire
here among the stars

All of the books
the mysterious books
the indecipherable books
written and forgotten

Abandoned in attics
moldering in basements
hauled to the curbside
with all the trash

What shall be burned?
What shall be drowned?
What shall be rescued?
What shall be reclaimed?

ABOUT THE AUTHOR

NORMAN FINKELSTEIN is the author of eleven books of poetry and six books of literary criticism, and has written extensively about modern poetry and Jewish literature. Born in New York City in 1954, he received his B.A. from Binghamton University and his Ph.D. from Emory University. He is Emeritus Professor of English at Xavier University in Cincinnati, Ohio, where he has lived since 1980. More about his work can be found at Norman Finkelstein: Poetry & Poetics (https://sites.google.com/site/normanfinkelsteinpoetry/); his poetry review blog, Restless Messengers, can be found at http://poetryinreview.com.

Author photograph by Zach Barocas